step by step MICROWAVE cooking for boys & girls

by
Bonnie Aeschliman

Ideals Publishing Corp.
Nashville, Tennessee

CONTENTS

GETTING STARTED	4
BREAKFASTS TO BRAG ABOUT	9
MARVELOUS MAIN MEALS	18
VERSATILE VEGETABLES	27
SENSATIONAL SALADS	31
SUPER SANDWICHES	34
DAZZLING DESSERTS	43
SPECIAL MENUS	47
SMACKIN' GOOD SNACKS	54
INDEX	64

A Note to Parents:
This book is written for children ages 8 and up. There may be some difficult procedures such as slicing or chopping, in which you may want to assist your child. It is also suggested that you familiarize your child with your particular microwave oven to ensure safety in the kitchen.

Director of Publishing: Patricia Pingry
Managing Editor: Marybeth Owens
Cookbook Editor: Cornell M. Brellenthin
Copy Editors: Linda Robinson, Shelly Bowerman
Art Director: Patrick McRae
Photographer: Gerald Koser
Food Stylist: Lisa Landers
Typographer: Kim Kaczanowski

ISBN 0-8249-3049-5
Copyright © MCMLXXXV by Ideals Publishing Corporation.
All rights reserved.
Printed and bound in the United States of America.

Published by Ideals Publishing Corporation
Nelson Place, Elm Hill Pike
Nashville, Tennessee

Cover Photo:
Breakfast Burrito, page 12.

Photo Opposite: The Lunch Club, page 36;
Chocolate Pudding from a Mix, page 44.

GETTING STARTED

Playing it Safe

1. ALWAYS get permission before you cook and make sure an adult is nearby in case you run into a problem or need some assistance.
2. Have an adult teach you how to use your particular microwave. You will need to know how to open and close the door properly, how to program the time, and how to turn it on and off.
3. NEVER operate an empty microwave. If you want to practice using it, place a cup of water inside to absorb the microwave energy.
4. Metal cookware and metal utensils are not recommended for microwave use. Do not use aluminum foil or dishes and utensils with a metal trim.
5. Keep the inside of the microwave clean. Wipe up spills as they occur.
6. Eggs cannot be cooked in the shell. Microwave energy causes pressure to build up inside the egg shell, and it will explode.
7. Potatoes, tomatoes, egg yolks, and other foods with a skin or membrane must be pierced BEFORE they are microwaved. This allows the steam to escape and keeps them from exploding.
8. If food is cooked for a very short time in the microwave, usually the container does not get hot. However, if a recipe requires several minutes of cooking, the food can get very hot, which does make the container hot enough to cause a burn. Always be careful when removing food from the microwave, and use potholders, if necessary.
9. Also, be careful when removing the covering from a dish that has been microwaved for several minutes. Let it stand for a few minutes, then carefully lift the side farthest away from you. This keeps the steam from gushing into your face.
10. If a dish is covered with plastic wrap, use a sharp knife to make a couple of slits in the top, before lifting the side farthest away from you.

Avoid Possible Exposure to Microwave Energy

1. NEVER operate the microwave oven with the door open.
2. NEVER wedge an object in the oven door.
3. NEVER allow food or dirt to accumulate in the microwave; keep it neat with a clean damp cloth.
4. NEVER operate the microwave if it is damaged in any way. This includes a bent door, broken or loosened hinges and latches, broken door seals, or broken inside surfaces.
5. The microwave should be repaired only by a qualified repairman.

GETTING STARTED 5

Microwave Tips

About Cooking Time

The recipes in this book were tested using 650 and 700 watt microwave ovens. All power settings are on HIGH (full power). If your microwave is one with a lower wattage, you will need to adjust the cooking time. Often, the recipes in this book state a cooking time range, such as 1 to 2 minutes. This is because the time will vary for several reasons, including: the shape of the food, temperature of the food, etc. The stated cooking time is followed by a visual guide, such as: until an inserted toothpick comes out clean, until the cheese is melted, until the sauce is thickened, etc.

When and How to Cover for Microwave Cooking

Recipes in this book will tell you what you should use to cover a food for cooking. If it does not say to cover, then cook it uncovered.

WAXED PAPER allows steam to escape; lay it loosely over the food.

PAPER TOWELS are often used. They allow steam to escape and catch splatters. Some foods are cooked on paper towels to absorb excess moisture; use *white* paper towels only.

PLASTIC WRAP should be heavy duty and fit snuggly over the dish. *It must be vented to allow steam to escape;* pierce the top in a few places with a small sharp knife.

How to Turn or Rotate Dish

To cook foods evenly in the microwave, some are turned, or rotated. Some recipes require a *quarter-turn;* others require a *half-turn.*

You will need to remember how to make a *quarter-turn.*

You have three red apples and 1 green apple in a baking dish. If the green apple is in the 12 o'clock position, and you move it to the 3 o'clock position, you have turned, or rotated, the dish a *quarter-turn.* See the picture at the right.

You will also need to remember how to make a *half-turn.*

You have three red apples and 1 green apple in a baking dish. If the green apple is in the 12 o'clock position, and you move it to the 6 o'clock position, you have turned, or rotated, the dish a *half-turn.* See the picture at the right.

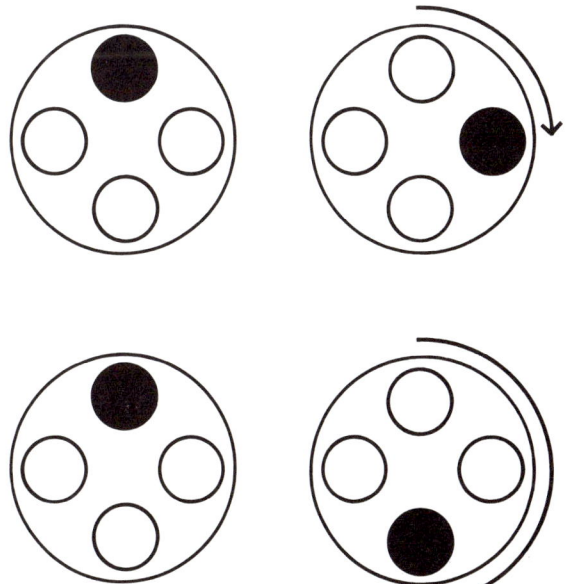

6 GETTING STARTED

Cooking Gear

For best results use the kind and size of utensil indicated in the recipe. The following equipment has been used extensively with children in mind.

Glass Utensils (See picture #1)

Batter Bowls are especially recommended for children. The handle makes it easy for the child to grasp, and it does not heat as rapidly as the sides of a bowl. Also, the spout aids in pouring liquids. Batter bowls come in 1-quart and 2-quart sizes.

Glass Baking Dishes are used in many recipes. They come in various sizes: 6 x 10 inches, 8 x 12 inches, 9 x 13 inches, and 9 x 9 inches. Try to use the size specified or you will have to adjust cooking time. Some glass baking dishes come with covers; this is very convenient, as you don't have to work with plastic wrap.

Round Casseroles come in different sizes: 1-quart, 1½-quart, 2-quart, and 3-quart. Many come with covers. If you use one without a lid and need to cover it, use plastic wrap and rememeber to vent it so steam will escape.

Glass Pie Plates come in various sizes; use the size specified in the recipe for best results. *Do not use metal pie plates in microwave ovens.*

Glass Measures are used to measure liquids, but they also make handy containers for microwaving. Several recipes will require these. Glass measures come in 1-cup, 2-cup, and 1-quart sizes.

Microwave Accessories (See picture #4)

Several companies make microwave accessories; these are particularly useful:

Microwave Ring Molds are excellent for dense foods such as meat loaf.

Microwave Muffin Pans are useful for microwaving muffins and cupcakes.

Crisper/Griddles are good for obtaining a crisp crust. They are very good for pizza and grilled sandwiches.

Measuring Equipment and Methods (See picture #2)

Dry Measure Cups are for measuring dry ingredients such as flour, sugar, brown sugar, cornstarch, and other dry ingredients. For most ingredients, just fill the measuring cup and level off with a spatula. Only brown sugar is measured differently; it is packed in, pressed down firmly, and then leveled off.

Glass Measures are used for measuring liquids. They have spouts for pouring liquids without spilling. To measure accurately, bend down so your eyes are level with the measurement mark you need. Slowly pour in the liquid. Stop when it reaches the right mark.

Measuring Spoons are used for measuring small amounts. Fill the spoon with the ingredient and level off with a spatula.

Butter and **Margarine** are very easy to measure; 1 stick is equal to ½ cup. Most wrappers are marked in tablespoons. All you need to do is place the butter on a small cutting board and cut through the wrapper and butter at the correct measurement line.

1. Glass Utensils

2. Measuring Equipment

3. Kitchen Gadgets

4. Microwave Accessories

GETTING STARTED

Kitchen Gadgets (See picture #3)

Wide metal spatula
Cooling rack
Paper cupcake liners
Plastic colander
Wire whisks

Small cutting board
Paring knife
Sandwich knife
Pizza cutter

Potholders
Wooden spoon
Rubber spatulas
Vegetable brush

Measuring Equivalents

3 Teaspoons	= 1	Tablespoon
½ Tablespoon	= 1½	Teaspoons
4 Tablespoons	= ¼	Cup
5 Tablespoons + 1 Teaspoon	= ⅓	Cup
16 Tablespoons	= 1	Cup
2 Cups	= 1	Pint
4 Cups or 2 Pints	= 1	Quart
4 Quarts	= 1	Gallon

Before You Cook

1. Read the recipe before you start.
2. Be a tidy cook. Wear an apron, tie back your hair if it is long, and wash your hands.
3. Get out the equipment listed in the recipe.
4. Measure the ingredients listed in the recipe.
5. Ask an adult to help you when cutting or chopping. Always cut down, with the knife blade toward the cutting board, and keep your fingers out of the way!
6. Keep your work area tidy. Put food away as soon as you are done with it, especially items that belong in the refrigerator. Clean up spills with a paper towel. Immediately, clean up anything spilled on the floor, so no one slips and falls.
7. Don't forget to clean up after you cook. Put everything away and leave a tidy kitchen. Show everyone that you are a responsible cook.

BREAKFASTS TO BRAG ABOUT

Breakfast Pizza

Makes 1 serving

INGREDIENTS:
- 1 pita round, 6 inches in diameter
- 1 teaspoon butter
- 1 egg
- 2 teaspoons water
- ¼ teaspoon dry minced onion
- 1 teaspoon Parmesan cheese
- 1 fully cooked sausage link, sliced
- Chopped green onion, optional
- Sliced mushrooms, optional
- Parsley flakes, optional
- ¼ cup shredded Cheddar cheese

EQUIPMENT:
- Measuring spoons and cups
- Crisper/griddle
- Small cutting board
- Dinner knife
- Plastic wrap
- 1-cup glass measure
- Fork
- Broad spatula
- Pizza cutter

1. Set the crisper/griddle in the microwave. Microwave on HIGH for 8 minutes. This makes the grill very hot so it will make a crispy crust.

2. While the crisper/griddle is heating, split the pita bread. Here's how: Place the pita bread on a small cutting board. Use a dinner knife to cut off a sliver along one edge. Now, insert your finger *or* the knife into the opening. Break bread apart at the seams. Go all the way around the edge until you come to the place where you began. Lift the bread apart, and you have two pieces. We will use only one for a single serving pizza. (Wrap the other one in plastic wrap and store in the refrigerator.)

3. When the crisper/griddle has heated for 8 minutes, using potholders, *carefully* remove it from the microwave by its handles. It will be very hot! Place one split pita round on the hot crisper/griddle, crust-side-down. Set aside while you prepare the egg mixture.

4. In a glass measure, microwave the butter for 20 to 30 seconds, until melted. Add the egg, water, onion, cheese, and sausage. Stir with a fork to mix well.

5. Microwave on HIGH for 30 seconds. Stir with a fork.

6. Microwave on HIGH for 15 seconds. Stir with a fork.

7. Microwave on HIGH for 5 to 15 seconds more, until the eggs begin to thicken. They should still be moist.

8. Spread eggs over the pita bread. If desired, top with onion, mushrooms, or parsley. Sprinkle with Cheddar cheese.

9. Carefully return the crisper/griddle back to the microwave and microwave on HIGH for 15 to 30 seconds, until the cheese melts. Very carefully remove the crisper/griddle. With a broad spatula transfer the pizza to a cutting board. Cut into wedges with a pizza cutter.

BREAKFASTS TO BRAG ABOUT

Walking Breakfast

Makes 1 serving

INGREDIENTS:
- 1 8-inch flour tortilla
- 2 to 3 tablespoons peanut butter
- 2 to 3 tablespoons grape jelly
- 1 small banana, peeled

EQUIPMENT:
- Paper towel
- Table knife

1. Place tortilla on a paper towel. Microwave 10 to 20 seconds on HIGH until the tortilla is soft and warm.
2. Spread with peanut butter.
3. Top with grape jelly.
4. Place the banana near the right edge of the tortilla.
5. Fold up the bottom one-fourth of the tortilla.
6. Bring right edge over the banana and roll up.

Crisp Bacon Slices

Makes 2 servings

INGREDIENTS:
- 4 slices bacon

EQUIPMENT:
- Paper towels
- 12 x 8-inch glass baking dish
- Plate
- Fork

1. Place 2 layers of paper towels in the glass dish.
2. Place bacon slices on top.
3. Cover bacon with another paper towel.
4. Microwave bacon on HIGH for 2 minutes 45 seconds to 3½ minutes, until golden and crisp.
5. Carefully remove the dish from microwave. Push the top towel back with a fork.
6. Line a plate with a clean paper towel. With a fork, carefully transfer cooked bacon to the towel-lined plate. This will absorb any excess grease.

Fruit Kebob

Makes 1 serving

INGREDIENTS:
- 3 banana slices, (½ inch thick)
- 3 strawberries
- 3 grapes
- 1 pineapple chunk
- 1 maraschino cherry

EQUIPMENT:
- One 6-inch wooden skewer

1. Stick the banana slices, strawberries, and grapes, in any order, on the wooden skewer.
2. Decorate the end of the skewer with a pineapple chunk and maraschino cherry.

Walking Breakfast, Crisp Bacon Slices, this page.

12 BREAKFASTS TO BRAG ABOUT

Breakfast Burrito

Makes 1 burrito

INGREDIENTS:
- 1 tablespoon butter
- 2 eggs
- 1 tablespoon water
- 1 10-inch flour tortilla
- 2 tablespoons shredded Cheddar cheese
- 1 tablespoon bacon bits
- 1 tablespoon mild picante sauce

EQUIPMENT:
- 2-cup glass measure
- Tablespoon
- Fork
- Paper towel
- Microwave-safe plate
- Napkin

1. Put butter in the glass measure. Microwave on HIGH for 30 to 40 seconds, until it is melted. Remove from the microwave.
2. Crack eggs into the glass measure. Add water; stir with a fork until well blended. Microwave on HIGH for 30 seconds. Stir well with a fork. Again, microwave on HIGH for 20 seconds. Stir well with a fork. Microwave on HIGH for another 15 to 30 seconds until eggs are done. (Eggs will look very soft and moist when they are done, but they will become firmer during standing time.)
3. Remove eggs from microwave. Cover with a paper towel. Let stand 1 to 2 minutes, until firm.
4. Place a flour tortilla between two paper towels, and set on plate. Microwave on HIGH for 10 seconds, to warm the tortilla. Remove from microwave and throw away top paper towel.
5. Form a line of scrambled eggs in the middle of the flour tortilla. Sprinkle with shredded cheese. Put bacon bits over the cheese. Drizzle picante sauce over everything — add a little more if you really like it; a little less if it is too spicy for you!
6. Fold up the bottom one-fourth of the tortilla. Fold it into thirds by bringing the right edge over to cover the eggs, then the left edge over.
7. To serve, wrap with a napkin and eat it as a sandwich.

Hot Chocolate

Makes 1 serving

INGREDIENTS:
- 2 tablespoons chocolate syrup
- ¾ cup milk
- 1 marshmallow

EQUIPMENT:
- Measuring spoons
- Glass *or* ceramic mug
- Teaspoon

1. Pour chocolate syrup in a glass mug.
2. Add milk. Stir with a teaspoon, until it is mixed.
3. Microwave on HIGH for 45 seconds.
4. Add the marshmallow. Microwave on HIGH for 15 to 30 seconds, until hot. Serve immediately.

BREAKFASTS TO BRAG ABOUT 13

Topsy Turvy Apple Pancake

Makes 6 servings

INGREDIENTS:
- 2 tablespoons butter
- 1 can (20 ounces) apple pie filling
- 2 tablespoons brown sugar
- 1 tablespoon lemon juice
- 1 teaspoon apple pie spice
- 1 cup complete pancake mix
- ¾ cup water
- 2 tablespoons brown sugar
- ¼ teaspoon cinnamon

EQUIPMENT:
- 9-inch microwave-safe pie plate
- Measuring cups and spoons
- 2 small mixing bowls
- Wooden spoon
- Waxed paper
- Potholders
- Wire whisk
- Small bowl *or* custard cup
- Toothpick
- Serving spatula

1. In the pie plate, microwave butter on HIGH for 15 to 20 seconds, just until melted. Tilt the pan so the butter spreads evenly over the bottom.

2. Put the apple pie filling in a small mixing bowl. Add the brown sugar, lemon juice, and apple pie spice. Stir with a wooden spoon to mix ingredients. Pour the mixture over the butter in the pie plate. Cover with a piece of waxed paper and microwave on HIGH for 2½ to 3½ minutes, until the apples are very hot. Remove from microwave with potholders.

3. In a small mixing bowl, combine pancake mix and water. Stir with a whisk until smooth. Pour the batter evenly over cooked apples.

4. In a small bowl, combine the brown sugar and cinnamon; sprinkle over the batter.

5. Microwave pancake on HIGH for 2 minutes. Rotate the dish a half-turn and microwave 2 to 3 minutes more, or until a toothpick inserted about 2 inches from the edge of the dish comes out clean.

6. With potholders, carefully remove from microwave. Let stand 5 minutes. Cut into 6 wedges and turn the wedges upside down with a serving spatula to serve.

Sugar 'n Spice Grapefruit

Makes 2 servings

INGREDIENTS:
- 1 grapefruit
- 1 tablespoon brown sugar
- ¼ teaspoon cinnamon
- 2 maraschino cherries

EQUIPMENT:
- Small cutting board
- Small knife
- Measuring spoon
- Small dish
- Paper plate

1. On cutting board, cut the grapefruit in half with a small knife; loosen each section so it is easier to eat. Remove any seeds and the middle pith from the fruit.

2. Combine the brown sugar and cinnamon in a small dish; sprinkle it over the grapefruit halves.

3. Place grapefruit halves on a paper plate. Microwave on HIGH for 1½ to 2 minutes, until heated through.

4. Decorate each with a cherry in the middle. Serve warm.

BREAKFASTS TO BRAG ABOUT

Scrambled Eggs

Makes 1 serving

INGREDIENTS:
- 1 tablespoon butter
- 2 eggs
- 1 tablespoon milk
- Salt to taste

EQUIPMENT:
- 2-cup glass measure
- Measuring spoons
- Fork
- Paper towel
- Serving plate

1. Put butter in the glass measure. Microwave on HIGH for 30 to 40 seconds, until it is melted. Remove from the microwave.
2. Crack eggs into the glass measure. Add milk; stir with a fork until well blended.
3. Microwave on HIGH for 30 seconds. Remove and stir with a fork.
4. Microwave on HIGH for 20 seconds. Remove and stir with a fork.
5. Microwave on HIGH for another 15 to 30 seconds, until the eggs are done. (The eggs will look very soft and moist when they are done, but they will become firmer during standing time.)
6. Remove eggs from microwave. Cover with a paper towel. Let stand 1 to 2 minutes, until firm.
7. Place on serving plate. Sprinkle with a bit of salt.

Egg Ragamuffin

Makes 1 serving

INGREDIENTS:
- 1 teaspoon butter
- 1 egg
- 1 teaspoon water
- 1 English muffin, split and toasted
- 1 thin slice cooked ham
- Salt and pepper
- 1 teaspoon mustard

EQUIPMENT:
- 2-cup glass measure
- Measuring spoons
- Fork
- Paper towel

1. Microwave butter in glass measure on HIGH for 20 to 30 seconds, until melted. Swirl butter around to grease the sides of the glass measure.
2. Add egg and water; blend lightly with a fork. Microwave on HIGH for 20 seconds. Stir with a fork.
3. Microwave on HIGH for 15 seconds. Stir again with a fork. If egg is not quite done, microwave on HIGH for 10 to 15 seconds more, until done. Egg will look moist even when it is done.
4. Remove from microwave. Let stand 1 minute.
5. Place English muffin on a paper towel. Fold the ham slice to fit on the bottom of the English muffin.
6. Slide the egg out and onto the ham. Salt and pepper to taste.
7. Spread mustard on the top half of the muffin, and place it over the egg. Wrap sandwich in a paper towel and microwave on HIGH for 10 to 15 seconds, until ham is warmed.

Egg Ragamuffin, this page; Fruit Kebob, page 11.

16 BREAKFASTS TO BRAG ABOUT

Apple Honeys

Makes 4 servings

INGREDIENTS:

- 4 medium cooking apples (such as Jonathan, Winesap, *or* Rome Beauty)
- ⅓ cup granola (commercially prepared *or* use the recipe on page 57)
- ¼ cup raisins
- ¼ cup chopped walnuts
- ½ teaspoon cinnamon
- 2 tablespoons honey
- ½ cup orange juice
- ¼ cup honey
- 2 tablespoons butter

EQUIPMENT:

- Measuring cups and spoons
- Apple corer
- Vegetable parer
- 9-inch glass baking dish
- Small glass mixing bowl
- Fork
- Teaspoon
- 1-cup glass measure
- Plastic wrap
- Potholders
- Hot pad *or* cooling rack
- 4 serving plates

1. Wash the apples. Remove the cores with an apple corer. (To do this, press the apple corer into the stem end of the apple. Press all the way down. Twist the apple corer slightly, then pull it out. Discard core.)
2. Pare a strip around the top of each apple with a vegetable parer. (Strip should be about ½ inch from top.)
3. Set the apples in the baking dish.
4. Combine granola, raisins, walnuts, cinnamon, and honey in small mixing bowl. Toss with a fork until honey is mixed into the dry ingredients.
5. Use a teaspoon to spoon the mixture into the middle of each apple.
6. Combine orange juice, honey, and butter in the glass measure. Microwave on HIGH for 1½ to 2 minutes, until the butter melts. Blend with a fork. Slowly drizzle over the apples.
7. Cover dish with plastic wrap. Turn back one corner so the steam can escape.
8. Microwave the apples on HIGH for 4 minutes. Turn the dish a half-turn.
9. Microwave on HIGH for 3 to 5 minutes more, until the apples are tender.
10. Using potholders, carefully remove the dish from the microwave. Set on a hot pad.
11. Let apples stand for 5 minutes before removing the plastic wrap.
12. Serve warm or cool on individual plates, with some of the sauce spooned over each apple.

BREAKFASTS TO BRAG ABOUT 17

Go Power Muffins

Makes 1 dozen

INGREDIENTS:

- 1 box (13 ounces) blueberry muffin mix
- 2 tablespoons wheat germ
- ¼ cup dates
- ¼ cup chopped walnuts
- ½ cup water
- 2 tablespoons oil
- 1 egg

TOPPING:

- 1 tablespoon blueberry muffin mix
- 1½ teaspoons cinnamon
- ⅓ cup brown sugar
- 1 teaspoon wheat germ

EQUIPMENT:

Strainer
1-quart mixing bowl
Measuring cups and spoons
Fork
2-cup measure
Microwave-safe muffin pan
Paper cupcake liners
Small mixing bowl
Toothpick
Cooling rack

1. Remove the can of blueberries from the box of mix. Drain the blueberries in a strainer over the sink. Wash them by holding the strainer under cold running water. This removes the juice and keeps the muffins from turning purple. Set aside.

2. Pour muffin mix into the mixing bowl. Remove 1 tablespoon of mix and set aside. Break up any lumps in the mix with a fork. Add the wheat germ, dates, and nuts. Stir to mix well.

3. Mix water, oil, and egg in the 2-cup measure. Blend well with a fork; add to the muffin mix. Stir until ingredients are moistened. Fold in blueberries.

4. Line muffin pan with two paper liners in each cup. This helps to absorb extra moisture. Fill each paper liner only half full.

5. Now make the topping; in the small bowl, combine the 1 tablespoon dry muffin mix, cinnamon, brown sugar, and wheat germ. Mix it well.

6. Spoon 1 teaspoon of topping on top of each unbaked muffin.

7. Microwave the muffins on HIGH for 60 seconds. Rotate the pan a quarter-turn.

8. Microwave the muffins 30 seconds. Rotate the pan a quarter turn. Microwave the muffins 15 to 30 seconds or until a toothpick inserted in the center comes out clean. The muffins may still look moist on top even though they are done. Carefully remove the pan from the microwave. Take the cupcakes out of the muffin pan and place on a cooling rack. Let them stand 5 minutes.

9. Line the same muffin pan with paper liners as before. Fill and bake again.

MARVELOUS MAIN MEALS

Wild West Chili

Makes 6 servings

INGREDIENTS:

- 1 pound lean ground beef
- 1 package (1¼ ounces) chili seasoning
- 1 can (10¾ ounces) tomato soup
- ⅓ cup water
- 1 can (15 ounces) chili beans

EQUIPMENT:

- 2-quart batter bowl *or* large glass bowl
- Paper towels
- Wooden spoon
- Potholders

1. Place ground beef in the batter bowl. Cover with a paper towel. Microwave on HIGH for 5 to 7 minutes, until meat is no longer pink. Stir meat once or twice during cooking with a wooden spoon so that it will cook evenly.
2. With potholders, *carefully* remove the bowl from the oven.
3. Add chili seasoning; stir with a wooden spoon to mix.
4. Add tomato soup, water, and chili beans. Stir to combine the ingredients.
5. Cover the bowl with a paper towel, and microwave on HIGH for 5 minutes. Stir with a wooden spoon.
6. Microwave on HIGH for another 4 to 6 minutes, until chili is simmering.
7. With potholders, *carefully* remove from oven. Let stand 5 minutes before serving.

Zesty Drumsticks

Makes 3 to 4 servings

INGREDIENTS:

- ¾ cup cornflake crumbs
- ¼ cup grated Parmesan cheese
- ½ teaspoon Italian herb seasoning
- ¾ teaspoon seasoned salt
- 6 chicken drumsticks, about 1¼ pounds

EQUIPMENT:

- Measuring cups and spoons
- Large plastic food bag
- Microwave-safe plate
- Paper towels
- Bowl
- Potholders, optional

1. Combine crumbs, cheese, herb seasoning, and salt in the food bag. Twist top and shake bag to mix the ingredients.
2. Line a plate with 2 paper towels.
3. Place the chicken pieces in a bowl and cover with cold water. Remove chicken from water and drop in the bag of crumbs. Shake bag to coat chicken. Place chicken on the paper towels. Arrange the drumsticks like the spokes of a wheel with the small ends toward the center of the plate.
4. Cover with a paper towel. Microwave on HIGH for 5 minutes. Rotate the plate a half-turn.
5. Microwave on HIGH 5 to 6 minutes, until the chicken is done. *Carefully* remove chicken from microwave. Let stand 4 to 5 minutes before serving.

Wild West Chili, this page.

MARVELOUS MAIN MEALS

Chicken and Rice

Makes 4 servings

INGREDIENTS:
- ¾ cup long-grain rice
- 1 can (10¾ ounces) cream of chicken soup
- 1½ cups milk
- ¼ cup chopped green pepper
- 1 jar (2 ounces) diced pimientos
- ½ cup chopped celery
- 1 jar (2½ ounces) sliced mushrooms
- 1 tablespoon instant chopped onion
- 6 chicken drumsticks
- 1 tablespoon dried parsley flakes
- Paprika

EQUIPMENT:
- 12 x 8-inch glass baking dish
- Wooden spoon
- Plastic wrap
- Small paring knife
- Potholders

1. Combine rice, soup, milk, green pepper, pimientos, celery, mushrooms, and onion in baking dish. Stir with wooden spoon to mix.
2. Arrange the drumsticks on top of the rice with the small ends pointing toward the center.
3. Sprinkle with parsley and paprika.
4. Cover the casserole with plastic wrap; smooth it on tightly. Then use the knife to make 4 or 5 slits in the plastic so steam can escape.
5. Microwave on HIGH for 20 minutes. Rotate the dish a half-turn. Microwave on HIGH for 10 to 15 minutes more, until liquid is absorbed.
6. Use potholders to remove casserole from oven. The dish will be hot! Let the casserole stand, covered, for 10 minutes before serving.
7. When removing the plastic wrap, uncover the side farthest from you first, so the steam will not burn you!

Italian Squiggles

Makes 6 servings

INGREDIENTS:
- 1 pound lean ground beef
- 1 jar (15½ ounces) Italian spaghetti sauce
- 2½ cups water
- 8 ounces corkscrew-shaped pasta
- Parmesan cheese, grated, optional

1. Set colander over the batter bowl. Place ground beef in the colander. Cover with a paper towel. Microwave on HIGH for 3 minutes. Stir with a wooden spoon to break up clumps.
2. Microwave on HIGH 2 to 3 minutes more, until the meat is no longer pink. Carefully remove the bowl and colander from the microwave. Set the colander of meat on a paper towel. Pour the meat drippings into a container to be discarded. Empty the colander of meat into the emptied batter bowl.

(Continued on next page)

MARVELOUS MAIN MEALS 21

EQUIPMENT:
- Plastic colander
- 2-quart microwave-safe batter bowl
- Paper towels
- Wooden spoon
- Measuring cups
- Waxed paper
- Potholders

3. Add spaghetti sauce and water to the meat. Microwave on HIGH for 6 to 7 minutes, until it is boiling.
4. Add the pasta. Cover with a piece of waxed paper. Microwave on HIGH for 5 minutes. Stir with a wooden spoon. Cover again with waxed paper.
5. Microwave on HIGH for 5 minutes. Stir again with a wooden spoon.
6. Microwave on HIGH 5 to 6 minutes, until pasta is tender.
7. With potholders, remove Italian Squiggles from the microwave - *the bowl will be very hot.*
8. Let Italian Squiggles stand for 5 minutes, then sprinkle with cheese, if desired.

Old Wagon Wheel Dinner

Makes 4 to 6 servings

INGREDIENTS:
- 1 can (16 ounces) pork and beans
- 1 can (8½ ounces) green lima beans, drained
- 1 can (15 ounces) kidney beans, drained
- 2 tablespoons instant minced onion
- ⅓ cup firmly packed brown sugar
- 1 tablespoon mustard
- 2 tablespoons barbecue sauce
- 6 frankfurters

EQUIPMENT:
- 2-quart glass casserole dish
- Wooden spoon
- Small cutting board
- Paring knife
- Plastic wrap
- Potholders

1. Combine all ingredients except frankfurters in the casserole dish. Stir with a wooden spoon to mix.
2. Place frankfurters on a small cutting board. Make diagonal slashes on top of each frankfurter, cutting only about ¼ inch deep. Cut each frankfurter in half, making 12 pieces.
3. Arrange frankfurters over casserole like the spokes of a wheel. Cover with plastic wrap; turn back one corner for steam to escape.
4. Microwave on HIGH for 12 to 15 minutes, until beans are bubbly and hot all the way through. Rotate dish once during cooking time.
5. With potholders, carefully remove from oven. Let stand for 4 to 5 minutes.

22 MARVELOUS MAIN MEALS

Super Supper Nachos

Makes 6 servings

INGREDIENTS:
- 1 pound lean ground beef
- 1 package (1¼ ounces) taco seasoning mix
- ⅓ cup water
- 1 can (16 ounces) refried beans
- 1 package (8 ounces) shredded Cheddar cheese
- 1 carton (8 ounces) sour cream
- ¼ cup sliced black olives
- 2 green onions, sliced
- Round tortilla chips

EQUIPMENT:
- 2-quart batter bowl *or* 2-quart glass bowl
- Paper towel
- Wooden spoon
- 6 x 10-inch glass baking dish

1. Place ground beef in batter bowl. Cover with a paper towel. Microwave on HIGH 3 minutes. Stir with a wooden spoon. Microwave 2 to 4 minutes more, until meat is no longer pink. Remove from the oven.
2. Stir in taco seasoning mix and water. Set aside.
3. Spread the beans in the bottom of the glass baking dish.
4. Evenly spread the meat mixture over the refried beans.
5. Sprinkle with shredded cheese.
6. Microwave on HIGH for 3 to 5 minutes, until the cheese is melted. Carefully remove from the oven.
7. Spread sour cream down the middle only. Sprinkle olive slices and onion slices over the sour cream.
8. Decorate with tortilla chips; stand them around the edge of the casserole. Makes it handy for dipping!
9. Serve additional tortilla chips in a basket on the side.

Garlic Bread

Makes 1 loaf

INGREDIENTS:
- ½ cup butter
- ½ teaspoon garlic powder
- 1 tablespoon dried parsley flakes
- 1 (1 pound) loaf French bread, sliced

EQUIPMENT:
- 1-cup glass measure
- Measuring spoons
- Pastry brush
- Napkins
- Basket *or* microwave-safe plate

1. In the glass measure, microwave butter on HIGH for 30 to 45 seconds, until melted.
2. Stir in garlic powder and parsley.
3. Brush butter on one side of bread slices.
4. Place bread in napkin-lined basket or on plate. Microwave on HIGH for 1 minute and 30 seconds, or until heated through.

Gold Nuggets with Honey Dip and Barely Barbecue Dip, page 24.

24 MARVELOUS MAIN MEALS

Gold Nuggets

Makes 2 servings

INGREDIENTS:
- 1 pound boneless and skinless chicken breast, halved
- ¾ cup milk
- 1 cup cornflake crumbs
- ⅓ cup grated Parmesan cheese
- ½ teaspoon seasoned salt
- ¼ teaspoon black pepper
- Honey Dip *or* Barely Barbecue Dip (recipes follow)

EQUIPMENT:
- Small cutting board
- Knife
- Medium bowl
- Measuring cups and spoons
- Plastic food storage bag
- Large microwave-safe plate
- Paper towels
- Potholders

1. Place chicken pieces on cutting board. Cut each one vertically to make 3 pieces. Then cut each strip horizontally to make 12 pieces. Try to keep the pieces the same size so they will cook evenly. Transfer the chicken to a mixing bowl.
2. Pour milk over chicken; set aside.
3. Pour the crumbs, cheese, salt, and pepper into a plastic bag; twist the top and shake it.
4. Line the plate with 2 or 3 layers of paper towels.
5. Drop about half the chicken pieces into the bag. Twist the top of the bag and shake it several times to coat the chicken pieces.
6. Arrange the chicken on the plate in a spoke-like pattern to make half a circle. The pieces may be close together, *but should not touch.*
7. Drop the remaining chicken into the bag. Twist and shake again.
8. Arrange on the plate to complete the circle. Cover with a paper towel. Microwave on HIGH for 5 minutes. Rotate the plate a half-turn.
9. Microwave on HIGH another 3 to 4 minutes, until the chicken is done.
10. With potholders, remove the plate from the oven. Let stand 5 minutes before serving. Make sauces while chicken is resting.

Honey Dip

Makes ¾ cup

INGREDIENTS:
- ½ cup honey
- 2 teaspoons lemon juice

EQUIPMENT:
- 1-cup glass measure
- Measuring spoons

1. Measure honey into glass measure. Add lemon juice.
2. Microwave on HIGH for 45 to 60 seconds, until hot.
3. Carefully remove from the microwave. Serve with Gold Nuggets.

MARVELOUS MAIN MEALS 25

Barely Barbecue Dip

Makes 1 cup

INGREDIENTS:
- ½ cup catsup
- ½ cup barbecue sauce

EQUIPMENT:
- 2-cup glass measure
- Wooden spoon

1. Pour catsup in glass measure.
2. Add barbecue sauce until it comes to the 1-cup measuring line on the measure.
3. Microwave on HIGH for 1 minute. Stir with wooden spoon.
4. Microwave on HIGH for 1 to 1½ minutes, until hot. Carefully remove from the microwave. Serve with Gold Nuggets.

Easy Meat Loaf Ring

Makes 4 servings

INGREDIENTS:
- 1 can (8 ounces) tomato sauce
- ¾ cup oats
- 2 tablespoons instant minced onion
- 1 teaspoon seasoned salt
- 2 teaspoons Worcestershire sauce
- 1 egg
- 1 pound lean ground beef
- ⅓ cup catsup

EQUIPMENT:
- Medium mixing bowl
- Measuring cups and spoons
- Fork
- Microwave ring mold *or* glass pie pan and custard cup*
- Paper towel
- Wooden spoon
- Potholders

1. Pour tomato sauce into mixing bowl.
2. Add oats, onion, salt, Worcestershire sauce, and egg; mix well.
3. Stir in the ground beef with a fork.
4. Pack meat loaf into the ring mold. Cover with a paper towel.
5. Microwave on HIGH for 6 minutes. Rotate dish about a quarter-turn.
6. Spoon catsup over top of meat loaf. Microwave on HIGH another 5 to 8 minutes.
7. With potholders, carefully remove meat loaf from oven. Let stand 5 minutes before serving.

*NOTE: If you do not have a microwave ring mold, use a glass pie plate and custard cup to create one. Here's how!
1. Put meat loaf mixture into pie plate and shape it into a firm, round ball. Flatten the top.
2. With the handle of a wooden spoon, poke a hole in the middle of the mound. Go 'round and 'round with the handle until you have a good-sized hole in the middle.
3. Set an empty glass *or* custard cup in the hole. Cover with a paper towel and microwave the same as above.

VERSATILE VEGETABLES

Space Spuds

Makes 4 to 6 servings

INGREDIENTS:
- 1 box (5½ ounces) Au Gratin Potatoes
- 2½ cups water
- ⅔ cup milk
- 1 tablespoon butter
- 2 teaspoons dried parsley flakes
- 1 teaspoon bacon bits

EQUIPMENT:
- 2-quart microwave-safe casserole with cover
- 1-quart glass measure
- Wire whisk
- Wooden spoon
- Potholders
- Measuring spoons
- Custard cup *or* small dish

1. Empty potatoes into casserole dish.
2. Combine water, milk, and butter in the glass measure. Sprinkle the envelope of seasoning mix into the liquid; whisk briskly to combine the ingredients.
3. Microwave on HIGH for 3½ to 4½ minutes, until boiling.
4. Carefully pour the liquid over the potatoes.
5. Cover and microwave on HIGH for 5 minutes. Carefully uncover and stir with a wooden spoon. Replace the cover.
6. Microwave on HIGH for 5 minutes. Carefully uncover and stir again. Replace the cover.
7. Microwave on HIGH for 6 minutes. Carefully remove from the microwave, using potholders if necessary. Let stand, covered, 4 to 5 minutes.
8. Combine parsley and bacon bits in a custard cup and sprinkle over the casserole.

Green Beans in a Snap

Makes 4 servings

INGREDIENTS:
- 1 can (16 ounces) cut green beans, drained
- 2 tablespoons butter
- 2 teaspoons sugar
- ¼ teaspoon salt
- 2 tablespoons sliced almonds

EQUIPMENT:
- 1-quart microwave-safe casserole dish with cover
- Measuring spoons
- Wooden spoon
- Potholders

1. Empty beans in the casserole dish.
2. Add the butter, sugar, and salt.
3. Cover the dish. Microwave on HIGH for 2 minutes. Carefully uncover and stir the green beans with a wooden spoon.
4. Cover again and microwave on HIGH for 1 to 2 minutes more, until beans are hot and the butter has melted.
5. Carefully remove from the microwave, using potholders. Let stand, covered, for 2 minutes. Carefully remove the cover, tilting it away from you. Stir the green beans, and sprinkle with almonds.

Corn on the Cob, Broccoli — Gee Whiz, page 28.

VERSATILE VEGETABLES

Broccoli— Gee Whiz!

Makes 4 servings

INGREDIENTS:
 1 package (10 ounces) frozen broccoli spears
 Cheese Sauce (recipe follows)

EQUIPMENT:
 1-quart microwave-safe casserole with cover
 Potholders, optional

1. Place broccoli in a covered casserole. Microwave on HIGH for 4 minutes; rotate a half-turn.
2. Microwave on HIGH for 2 minutes more; carefully remove from microwave.
3. Let broccoli stand covered for 5 minutes before serving. Make Cheese Sauce and pour over cooked broccoli spears.

Cheese Sauce

Makes 1 cup

INGREDIENTS:
 1 cup milk
 2 tablespoons cornstarch
 ¼ teaspoon salt
 1 tablespoon butter
 1 cup (4 ounces) shredded American cheese *or* Cheddar cheese

EQUIPMENT:
 2-cup glass measure
 Measuring spoons and cups
 Small whisk
 Rubber spatula

1. Pour milk into glass measure. Add cornstarch and salt; whisk to combine and to dissolve any lumps. Add the butter.
2. Microwave on HIGH 1½ minutes; whisk well.
3. Microwave on HIGH for 30 seconds. The sauce will start to thicken near the edges. Whisk well.
4. Microwave on HIGH for 20 to 35 seconds, just until thickened.
5. Carefully remove from the microwave. With a rubber spatula, stir in the cheese. Let stand 1 or 2 minutes. Stir again to blend.
6. Serve Cheese Sauce over cooked broccoli spears or other cooked vegetables.

Corn on the Cob

Makes 4 servings

INGREDIENTS:
 4 ears frozen corn on the cob
 Butter
 Salt and pepper

EQUIPMENT:
 Large microwave-safe plate
 Plastic wrap
 Small paring knife
 Potholders

1. Arrange corn on the plate, like the spokes of a wheel.
2. Cover with plastic wrap. (You will need to use two strips to cover it completely.) Tuck the ends of the plastic wrap under the plate. Use a small sharp knife to make 3 or 4 slits in the plastic wrap.
3. Microwave on HIGH for 6 minutes; rotate the plate a half-turn.
4. Microwave on HIGH for 6 to 7 more minutes. Carefully remove from the microwave, using potholders. Let stand 3 minutes before serving.
5. Serve with butter, salt, and pepper.

VERSATILE VEGETABLES 29

Best Baked Beans

Makes 8 servings

INGREDIENTS:

- 2 strips bacon, cut in half
- 2 cans (16 ounces) pork and beans
- ⅓ cup brown sugar
- ¼ cup catsup
- 1 tablespoon dry minced onion
- 1 tablespoon mustard
- 1 teaspoon Worcestershire sauce

EQUIPMENT:

- 1½-quart microwave-safe casserole dish
- Paper towels
- Paper towel-lined plate
- Measuring cups and spoons
- Wooden spoon
- Potholders

1. Place bacon in the casserole dish.
2. Cover with a paper towel. Microwave on HIGH for 2 minutes, or until the bacon is golden and crisp.
3. Carefully remove from the microwave. Place the bacon on a paper towel-lined plate. Set aside.
4. Add the pork and beans to the bacon drippings in the casserole dish.
5. Add the brown sugar, catsup, onion, mustard, and Worcestershire sauce; stir with a wooden spoon.
6. Cover with a paper towel. Microwave on HIGH for 5 minutes; stir.
7. Microwave on HIGH for 4 to 5 minutes, until bubbling. Carefully remove from microwave, using potholders. Let stand 5 minutes.
8. Crumble the cooked bacon over the beans and serve.

Baked Potato

Makes 1 serving

INGREDIENTS:

- 1 medium potato
- 1 tablespoon butter
- 1 tablespoon sour cream
- 2 tablespoons shredded American *or* Cheddar cheese
- ½ teaspoon bacon bits

EQUIPMENT:

- Vegetable brush
- Fork
- Potholders
- Aluminum foil
- Paring knife
- Measuring spoons

1. Scrub the potato with a vegetable brush.
2. Use a fork to pierce the skin of the potato. Pierce both the top and the bottom!
3. Microwave on HIGH for 2 minutes. Turn the potato over and move it 2 or 3 inches in any direction. Microwave on HIGH for another 1½ to 2 minutes.
4. With potholders, remove the potato from the microwave; wrap it in a small square of aluminum foil, and let it stand 5 to 7 minutes.
5. To serve, cut an "X" in the top of the potato with a small paring knife. Gently squeeze in the ends of the potato to fluff it up.
6. Place the butter in the potato. Add sour cream. Sprinkle with shredded cheese and bacon bits.

SENSATIONAL SALADS

Unbelievable Salad

Makes 6 servings

INGREDIENTS:
- 1 can (15½ ounces) crushed pineapple
- 1 package (3 ounces) cherry flavored gelatin
- 1 can (11 ounces) mandarin oranges, drained
- 1 carton (8 ounces) creamed cottage cheese
- 1 carton (4½ ounces) frozen whipped topping, thawed
- Lettuce leaves

EQUIPMENT:
- 6-cup glass measure
- Potholders
- Wooden spoon
- 8-inch square dish

1. Pour the pineapple with its juice into a glass measure. Microwave on HIGH for 2 to 2½ minutes, until boiling. Carefully remove from microwave, using potholders.
2. Add the gelatin; stir with a wooden spoon until dissolved. Chill in the refrigerator until it is cool and begins to thicken; this will take about 2 hours.
3. Remove from refrigerator and stir in the oranges, cottage cheese, and whipped topping. Pour into the square dish. Refrigerate until firm.
4. Cut into squares and serve on lettuce leaves.

Double Red Salad

Makes 6 servings

INGREDIENTS:
- ¼ cup cinnamon candies
- ½ cup water
- 1 package (3 ounces) raspberry gelatin dessert
- 1 can (16 ounces) applesauce
- Lettuce leaves, optional
- Vanilla yogurt, optional

EQUIPMENT:
- Measuring cups
- 1-quart glass measure
- Potholders
- Wooden spoon
- 8-inch square glass dish

1. Combine the candies and water in a glass measure. Microwave on HIGH for 4 to 5 minutes, until the candies are dissolved. Carefully remove from microwave, using potholders.
2. Stir in the gelatin dessert with a wooden spoon; continue to stir until it is dissolved.
3. Add applesauce; stir to combine.
4. Pour into glass dish. Refrigerate several hours until set.
5. To serve, cut salad into 6 squares. If desired, place each square on a lettuce leaf, and top with vanilla yogurt.

Unbelievable Salad, this page.

32 SENSATIONAL SALADS

Berry Good Salad

Makes 8 servings

INGREDIENTS:
- 3 tablespoons cornstarch
- ½ cup sugar
- 1¼ cups lemon-lime soft drink
- 4 to 6 drops red food coloring
- 1 quart fresh strawberries
- 2 medium bananas, peeled
- Lettuce leaves

EQUIPMENT:
- Measuring cups
- 1-quart batter bowl
- Wire whisk
- Wooden spoon
- Potholders
- Paper towels
- Small cutting board
- Small knife

1. Combine cornstarch and sugar in batter bowl; stir to mix.
2. Whisk in the soft drink. Microwave on HIGH for 1 minute and stir.
3. Microwave on HIGH for 1 minute; stir with a wooden spoon.
4. Microwave on HIGH for 30 to 60 seconds, until boiling and the mixture becomes thick and clear. Carefully remove from the microwave, using potholders.
5. Add enough food coloring to give it a pretty rosy pink color; whisk well. Let stand to cool at room temperature.
6. Rinse the strawberries in cold water; *do not soak*. Remove the stems.
7. Place strawberries with the pointed ends up on a paper towel.
8. On a cutting board, cut bananas into ¾-inch slices.
9. Carefully fold the bananas and strawberries into the thickened pink mixture. Refrigerate until serving time.
10. Serve on lettuce leaves as a salad, or in pretty dishes for a dessert.

Fruit 'n Bubbles

Makes 6 servings

INGREDIENTS:
- 1 package (3¼ ounces) tapioca pudding mix
- 1 can (8 ounces) pineapple chunks
- ⅔ cup orange juice
- ¾ cup milk
- 1 can (11 ounces) mandarin oranges, drained
- 1 large banana, peeled
- Lettuce leaves, optional

1. Empty the pudding mix into a batter bowl.
2. Drain the can of pineapple over a 1-cup measure. There will be about ⅓ cup juice. Add enough orange juice to make 1 cup. Add to the pudding mix.
3. Add milk; stir with wooden spoon to combine. Microwave on HIGH for 3½ minutes. Stir well.
4. Microwave on HIGH for 1 minute; stir.
5. Microwave on HIGH for 1½ minutes, or until mixture comes to a full boil. Stir again.
6. Let stand at room temperature for 15 minutes, stirring twice.

(Continued on next page)

SENSATIONAL SALADS 33

EQUIPMENT:
 1-quart batter bowl
 Measuring cups
 Wooden spoon
 Small cutting board
 Paring knife
 Plastic wrap

7. Stir in pineapple chunks and oranges.
8. On a small cutting board, slice banana into thick slices; add to the pudding and stir.
9. Cover with plastic wrap and chill.
10. Serve on lettuce leaves as a salad or in pretty glasses as dessert.

Marinated Bean Salad

Makes 8 to 10 servings

INGREDIENTS:
 1 can (16 ounces) cut green beans, drained
 1 can (16 ounces) yellow wax beans, drained
 1 can (15 ounces) kidney beans, drained
 1 can (8½ ounces) green lima beans, drained
 ½ cup chopped green pepper
 ½ cup sugar
 ½ cup vinegar
 ⅓ cup salad oil
 1 tablespoon dry minced onion
 1 teaspoon seasoned salt
 1 teaspoon celery seed
 ¼ teaspoon pepper

EQUIPMENT:
 2-quart glass bowl
 Measuring cups and spoons
 2-cup glass measure
 Potholders
 Teaspoon
 Wooden spoon

1. In a glass bowl, combine the green beans, wax beans, kidney beans, lima beans, and green pepper. Set aside.
2. In a glass measure, combine the sugar, vinegar, oil, onion, seasoned salt, celery seed, and pepper. Microwave on HIGH for 1½ to 2 minutes, until boiling.
3. Carefully remove from the microwave, using potholders. Stir with a teaspoon to combine all the ingredients.
4. Pour hot dressing over the beans. Stir with a wooden spoon.
5. Salad can be served immediately, or refrigerate for several hours and serve chilled.

SUPER SANDWICHES

Fish-n-Boats

Makes 2 servings

INGREDIENTS:
- 1 can (6 ounces) tuna, drained
- ½ cup mayonnaise
- ⅓ cup chopped celery
- ¼ cup sweet pickle relish, drained
- 2 large French rolls, about 6 inches long
- ½ cup shredded American cheese
- 1 slice American cheese
- 2 olives, sliced

EQUIPMENT:
- Measuring cups and spoons
- Small mixing bowl
- Fork
- Small cutting board
- Small knife
- Paper plates
- Paper towels
- 2 wooden skewers

1. Combine tuna, mayonnaise, celery, and pickle relish in mixing bowl. Stir well with a fork; set aside.
2. Place one French roll on a cutting board. Carefully cut a thin slice, lengthwise, off the top of the roll.
3. With your fingers, hollow out the roll by removing some of the soft bread; leave about a ½-inch shell. This makes the "boat" for the sandwich. Prepare the other roll the same way.
4. Line a paper plate with a paper towel. Place the "boats" on the plate.
5. Sprinkle 2 tablespoons of shredded cheese into each "boat."
6. Fill the "boats" with tuna mixture. Sprinkle with remaining shredded cheese.
7. Place a paper towel over the sandwiches; microwave on HIGH for 2 to 2½ minutes, until cheese is melted. Carefully remove from microwave.
8. Cut the slice of American cheese diagonally. Thread a wooden skewer through the cheese to make a sail. Place a sail in each "boat."
9. Top with sliced olives.

Ball Park Hot Dog

Makes 1 serving

INGREDIENTS:
- 1 hot dog
- 1 hot dog bun
- Mustard, optional
- Catsup, optional
- Pickle relish, optional

EQUIPMENT:
- Fork
- Napkin

1. With a fork, pierce skin of hot dog in 3 or 4 places. Place the hot dog in a bun and wrap loosely with a napkin.
2. Microwave on HIGH for 20 to 30 seconds.
3. Add mustard, catsup, or pickle relish, if you like.

Fish-n-Boats, this page

36 SUPER SANDWICHES

Dip 'n Sip

Makes 1 generous serving

INGREDIENTS:

 1 submarine roll, partially split
 2 tablespoons mayonnaise
 1 teaspoon mustard
 ¼ teaspoon horseradish
 ¼ pound sliced roast beef
  Salt and pepper, optional
 1 can (7¼ ounces) beef broth

EQUIPMENT:

 Paper towels
 Custard cup
 Measuring spoons
 Sandwich knife
 Can opener
 Microwave-safe mug

1. Place the roll on a paper towel. Open it so it will lay flat.
2. In a small custard cup, mix together the mayonnaise, mustard, and horseradish; spread over the roll.
3. Place the roast beef inside the roll. Salt and pepper, if desired.
4. Wrap a paper towel around the sandwich and microwave on HIGH for 45 to 60 seconds, until warm. Let stand 1 minute before serving.
5. Pour broth into a mug. Microwave on HIGH for 1 minute.
6. Cut sandwich in half and serve with broth.

The Lunch Club

Makes 1 serving

INGREDIENTS:

 2 slices bacon
 3 slices whole wheat bread
 2 tablespoons mayonnaise or Thousand Island dressing
 1 thin slice tomato
 2 lettuce leaves
 1 thin slice ham
 1 slice Swiss cheese

EQUIPMENT:

 Paper towels
 Paper plates
 Toaster
 Cutting board
 Measuring spoons
 Table knife
 4 frilled picks
 Sandwich knife
 Serving plate

1. Line a paper plate with two layers of paper towels. Place bacon on the towels. Cover with another paper towel. Microwave on HIGH for 1½ to 2½ minutes, until bacon is golden and crisp. Set aside.
2. While bacon is cooking, toast the bread.
3. Place toast on a cutting board; spread evenly with mayonnaise.
4. Break the bacon slices in half, making 4 pieces; place on the first piece of toast. Add a tomato slice and a lettuce leaf.
5. Top with the second piece of toast, mayonnaise-side-up. Add the ham, the cheese, and the last lettuce leaf. Top with the last piece of toast, mayonnaise-side-down.
6. Place a frilled pick through the sandwich at the top, one at the bottom, and one on each side.
7. Carefully cut sandwich from corner to corner to make 4 pieces. Arrange on a plate with cut edges up.

SUPER SANDWICHES   37

Coney Fiesta Dog

Makes 1 serving

INGREDIENTS:
- 1 hot dog
- 1 hot dog bun
- 2 tablespoons chili with beans
- 2 tablespoons shredded Cheddar cheese
- 1 tablespoon coarsely crushed tortilla chips

EQUIPMENT:
- Small cutting board
- Paring knife
- Small mixing bowl
- Measuring spoons
- Spoon
- Napkin

1. On a cutting board, partially split the hot dog lengthwise; be careful not to cut all the way through.
2. Place the hot dog in the hot dog bun.
3. In a small bowl, combine chili, cheese, and crushed tortilla chips. Stir to mix; spoon into the hot dog.
4. Wrap a napkin around the sandwich. Microwave on HIGH for 30 to 40 seconds, until the cheese is melted.

Fiesta Burgers

Makes 2 servings

INGREDIENTS:
- ½ pound lean ground beef
- 1 tablespoon taco seasoning mix
- 2 tablespoons mild taco sauce
- 2 hamburger buns
- Shredded cheese
- Shredded lettuce
- Chopped tomato
- Avocado dip
- Taco sauce

EQUIPMENT:
- Small mixing bowl
- Measuring spoons
- Fork
- Microwave-safe plate
- Paper towels
- Potholders, optional
- Wide spatula
- Napkins

1. In a small mixing bowl, combine the ground beef, taco seasoning mix, and taco sauce. Mix well with a fork.
2. Shape into two patties.
3. Line a plate with two or three layers of paper towels. Place the patties on the paper towels; cover with another paper towel. Microwave on HIGH for 2 minutes.
3. Give the plate a half-turn, and microwave on HIGH for another 1 to 2 minutes, until the burgers are done.
4. Carefully remove the burgers from the microwave, using potholders if necessary. Let the burgers stand for 2 or 3 minutes.
5. With a wide spatula, place each burger on a bun. Wrap in napkins; place both sandwiches on a plate. Microwave on HIGH for 20 to 25 seconds to warm the buns.
6. Top each Fiesta Burger with cheese, lettuce, and tomato. Serve with avocado dip and taco sauce.

38 SUPER SANDWICHES

Catch-of-the-Day

Makes 2 servings

INGREDIENTS:

  4 frozen fish sticks
  2 hamburger rolls
  ¼ cup tartar sauce
  ¼ cup slaw *or* ⅓ cup shredded lettuce

EQUIPMENT:

  Microwave-safe plate
  Paper towels
  Measuring cups and spoons
  Napkins

1. Line plate with a paper towel.
2. Arrange fish sticks in a spoke-like pattern on the paper towel. Cover with another paper towel. Microwave on HIGH for 1 minute. Let stand 2 minutes.
3. Microwave on HIGH for 1½ to 2 minutes more, until fish is cooked. Remove from microwave. Let stand 2 minutes.
4. Open rolls. Spread 1 tablespoon tarter sauce on top and bottom of each roll.
5. Place 2 tablespoons slaw on the bottom half of each roll.
6. Place 2 fish sticks over the slaw; add roll tops.
7. To warm, wrap each sandwich in a napkin. Place both sandwiches on a plate. Microwave on HIGH for 20 seconds and serve immediately.

Tacos

Makes 8 servings

INGREDIENTS:

  1 pound lean ground beef
  ¼ cup water
  1 package (1¼ ounces) taco seasoning mix
  8 crisp taco shells
  1 cup shredded Cheddar cheese
  1 cup shredded lettuce
  1 large tomato, diced

EQUIPMENT:

  2-quart batter bowl *or* 2-quart microwave-safe mixing bowl
  Paper towels
  Wooden spoon
  Potholders
  Container for excess grease
  1-cup glass measure

1. Place the ground beef in a batter bowl; cover with a paper towel. Microwave on HIGH for 5 to 6 minutes, until the meat is no longer pink. Stir the meat once or twice during cooking with a wooden spoon.
2. With potholders, remove the bowl; carefully drain excess fat into a container to be discarded.
3. Add water and taco seasoning mix. Stir with a wooden spoon.
4. Cover with a paper towel. Microwave on HIGH for 4 minutes. Stir. Microwave on HIGH for 1 or 2 minutes.
5. Spoon into taco shells. Top with shredded cheese, lettuce, and tomato.

Fiesta Burgers, page 3

40 SUPER SANDWICHES

Sloppy Joes

Makes 6 servings

INGREDIENTS:
- 1 pound lean ground beef
- ¼ cup chopped green pepper
- ½ teaspoon celery seed
- 1 can (10¾ ounces) tomato soup
- ¼ cup water
- 2 tablespoons dry minced onion
- 1 teaspoon mustard
- 6 hamburger rolls

EQUIPMENT:
- 2-quart batter bowl *or* 2-quart microwave-safe mixing bowl
- Paper towel
- Wooden spoon
- Potholders, optional
- Container for excess grease
- Measuring cups and spoons
- Plastic wrap

1. Place the ground beef in a batter bowl; cover with a paper towel. Microwave on HIGH for 5 to 6 minutes, until the meat is no longer pink. Stir the meat once or twice during cooking with a wooden spoon.
2. Carefully remove the bowl from the oven using potholders if necessary. Carefully drain excess grease into a container to be discarded.
3. Add the green pepper, celery seed, tomato soup, water, onion, and mustard. Stir to combine the ingredients.
4. Cover the bowl with plastic wrap; fold back one corner. Microwave on HIGH for 4 minutes. Stir. Microwave on HIGH for another 4 or 5 minutes.
5. Carefully remove the bowl. Let stand 5 minutes before serving.
6. To serve, spoon a generous amount into each hamburger roll.

Flash Burgers

Makes 2 servings

INGREDIENTS:
- ½ pound lean ground beef
- 1 teaspoon instant minced onion
- Salt and pepper
- 2 hamburger buns
- Salt and pepper, optional
- Pickle relish, optional
- Catsup, optional
- Mustard, optional

1. In a small mixing bowl, combine the ground beef and onion; shape into two hamburger patties.
2. Line a plate with two or three paper towels. Place the patties on the paper towels.
3. Cover with a paper towel and microwave on HIGH for 2 minutes.
4. Give the plate a quarter-turn; microwave on HIGH for another 1 to 2 minutes, until the burgers are done.
5. Carefully remove from the microwave, using potholders if necessary.

(Continued on next page)

SUPER SANDWICHES

EQUIPMENT:
- Small mixing bowl
- Microwave-safe plate
- Paper towels
- Potholders, optional
- Wide spatula
- Napkins

6. With a wide spatula, place each burger on a bun. Wrap in napkins and microwave on HIGH for 20 to 25 seconds. Remove from the microwave. Add salt and pepper if you like. Let stand 1 or 2 minutes.
7. Serve with pickle relish, catsup, or mustard, if desired.

Tower of Pizza

Makes 3 servings

INGREDIENTS:
- ½ teaspoon Italian herb seasoning
- ¼ teaspoon salt
- 1 egg
- ¼ cup dry bread crumbs
- ½ pound lean ground beef
- 1 can (10½ ounces) pizza sauce
- 3 submarine rolls, partially split
- 1½ cups shredded mozzarella cheese
- 1 jar (2½ ounces) sliced mushrooms
- 2 tablespoons chopped green pepper

EQUIPMENT:
- Measuring spoons and cups
- Small mixing bowl
- Fork
- Microwave-safe plates
- Paper towels
- Potholders
- Spoon
- Napkins

1. In a small mixing bowl, combine Italian seasoning, salt, egg, and dry bread crumbs. Mix well with a fork.
2. Add the ground beef; mix in completely with a fork or *very clean* hands.
3. Line a plate with two layers of paper towels.
4. With *clean hands,* shape meat into 9 meatballs.
5. Arrange meatballs in a circle on the plate. Cover with another paper towel.
6. Microwave on HIGH for 2 minutes. Rotate the plate a quarter-turn.
7. Microwave on HIGH for 1½ to 2 minutes, until done. With potholders, carefully remove from microwave. Let stand 2 or 3 minutes.
8. Spoon a tablespoon of pizza sauce on the bottom of each submarine roll. Sprinkle each with a tablespoon of mozzarella cheese.
9. Place 3 meatballs on each roll.
10. Spoon another 1 or 2 tablespoon of pizza sauce over meatballs.
11. Top with mushrooms and green peppers.
12. Sprinkle with remaining mozzarella cheese.
13. Cover sandwiches with the submarine roll tops.
14. Wrap each sandwich in a napkin. Place the sandwiches on a microwave-safe plate. Microwave on HIGH for 1 to 2 minutes, until cheese is melted.

DAZZLING DESSERTS

Strawberry Shortcakes

Makes 4 servings

INGREDIENTS:
- 4 individual dessert spongecakes
- 1 pint vanilla ice cream
- Strawberry Sauce (recipe below)
- Sliced almonds, optional

EQUIPMENT:
- 4 dessert plates
- Ice cream scoop
- Tablespoon

1. Place a spongecake on each dessert plate.
2. Top each with a generous scoop of vanilla ice cream.
3. Top with 2 or 3 tablespoons of Strawberry Sauce. Serve immediately. Decorate with almonds if you like.

TIP: If the Strawberry Sauce has been refrigerated, put about 1 cup of sauce in a 2-cup measure. Microwave on HIGH for 1 minute. Stir. Microwave on HIGH for 15 to 30 seconds, until warm. Stir and pour over ice cream.

Strawberry Sauce

Makes about 2 cups

INGREDIENTS:
- 1 package (16 ounces) frozen sliced strawberries
- ¼ cup sugar
- 2 tablespoons cornstarch
- ¼ cup strawberry jam

EQUIPMENT:
- 1-quart glass measure
- Fork
- Small mixing bowl
- Measuring spoons and cups
- Wooden spoon

1. Empty strawberries into a glass measure.
2. Microwave on HIGH for 1 minute. Break apart with a fork. Microwave on HIGH for 1 minute or until berries have thawed and can be broken apart. Stir with a fork; let stand for 5 minutes.
3. In a small bowl, combine the sugar and the cornstarch; mix well.
4. Pour the mixture into the berries; stir with wooden spoon. Microwave on HIGH for 1½ minutes; stir.
5. Microwave for 1 minute and stir.
6. Microwave for 1 minute; stir.
7. Microwave for 1 minute or until the mixture bubbles and boils. Remove from microwave and stir.
8. Add jam. Let stand 1 minute, then mix.
9. Serve warm over ice cream or cake. Refrigerate leftover sauce in a covered container and use it within a few days.

Strawberry Shortcakes, this page.

44 DAZZLING DESSERTS

Chocolate Pudding from a Mix
Makes 4 servings

INGREDIENTS:
- 1 box (3½ ounces) chocolate pudding mix, *do not use instant*
- 2 cups milk

EQUIPMENT:
- 1-quart batter bowl
- 2-cup measure
- Wire whisk
- Waxed paper *or* plastic wrap

1. Empty pudding mix into a batter bowl.
2. Whisk in milk.
3. Microwave on HIGH for 3 minutes. Whisk the mixture well.
4. Microwave on HIGH for 1 minute. Whisk well.
5. Microwave on HIGH for 1 minute. Whisk well.
6. Microwave on HIGH for 1 to 1½ minutes, until the mixture comes to a full boil. Whisk well.
7. Cover the pudding with waxed paper and refrigerate. To serve, spoon into dessert dishes.

Variations

- **Vanilla Pudding:** Substitute a 3½-ounce box vanilla pudding mix, *not instant*, for the chocolate pudding mix.
- **Butterscotch Pudding:** Substitute a 3½-ounce box of butterscotch pudding mix, *not instant*, for the chocolate pudding mix.

Cherry Crisp Cups
Makes 5 servings

INGREDIENTS:
- 1 can (21 ounces) cherry pie filling
- ½ cup firmly packed brown sugar
- ⅓ cup flour
- ⅓ cup oats
- 3 tablespoons butter
- Whipped cream, optional

EQUIPMENT:
- 5 custard cups
- Measuring cups
- Small mixing bowl
- Fork
- 1-cup glass measure
- Potholders, optional

1. Spoon pie filling evenly into 5 custard cups.
2. Combine brown sugar, flour, and oats in a small mixing bowl. Stir with a fork until blended.
3. Place butter in a glass measure. Microwave on HIGH for 20 to 30 seconds, until melted; pour into flour mixture. Toss with a fork until mixed.
4. Sprinkle evenly over the cherry pie filling.
5. Place the custard cups in a circle inside the microwave. Microwave on HIGH for 3½ minutes.
6. Give the cups a quarter-turn.
7. Microwave on HIGH for 2 to 3 minutes, until the tops are toasty and the cherry mixture bubbles.
8. Carefully remove from the microwave, using potholders, if necessary. Let cool for several minutes.
9. Serve warm or cold and decorate with whipped cream, if desired.

DAZZLING DESSERTS   45

Triple Chocolate Cupcakes
Makes 1 dozen

INGREDIENTS:
- 1 box (9 ounces) devil's food cake mix
- ⅓ cup water
- 1 egg
- 2 tablespoons vegetable oil
- ⅓ cup mini chocolate chips
- Fudgy Frosting (recipe follows) *or* prepared chocolate frosting

EQUIPMENT:
- 1-quart mixing bowl
- Measuring cups and spoons
- Wooden spoon
- Microwave 6-cup muffin pan
- Paper cupcake liners
- Cooling rack

1. In a mixing bowl, combine cake mix, water, egg, and oil. Stir until blended and no lumps remain.
2. Fold in the chocolate chips.
3. Line each muffin cup with 2 paper liners.
4. Evenly, fill each paper liner *half* full.
5. Microwave on HIGH for 30 seconds. Rotate the pan a half-turn.
6. Microwave for 30 to 60 seconds, or until a toothpick inserted in the center comes out clean. (Cupcakes may still look moist on the top even though they are done.) Carefully remove from the microwave. Transfer cupcakes from the muffin pan to a cooling rack. Let them stand 2 or 3 minutes.
7. Line the muffin pan again. Fill with remaining batter and bake as before.
8. Frost cooled cupcakes with Fudgy Frosting.

NOTE: If you do not have a microwave muffin pan, you can still make cupcakes by using 6 glass custard cups. Line each cup with 2 paper liners. Fill half full. Place the cups in a circle on a large microwave-safe plate. Bake for 30 seconds; rotate the plate a half turn, and proceed baking as the recipe directs.

Fudgy Frosting
Makes about ¾ cup

INGREDIENTS:
- 2 tablespoons butter
- 2 tablespoons milk
- 2 tablespoons cocoa
- 1 cup powdered sugar
- ½ teaspoon vanilla

EQUIPMENT:
- Measuring cups and spoons
- 1-quart glass measure
- Small mixing bowl
- Rubber spatula
- Table knife *or* small metal spatula

1. Combine butter, milk, and cocoa in a glass measure. Microwave on HIGH for 30 to 40 seconds, until the butter is melted.
2. Add powdered sugar; stir with a rubber spatula until mixed well.
3. Add vanilla; mix well.
4. Place about 1 tablespoon frosting on each cooled cupcake. Use a table knife to spread frosting.

SPECIAL MENUS

THE PIZZA PARTY
Pizza Planks (page 48)
Smart Snacks (page 47)   Wonder Dip (page 47)
Zebra Parfaits (page 48)
Soft Drinks

Smart Snacks with Wonder Dip

Makes 3 to 4 servings

INGREDIENTS:
- Assorted fresh vegetables
- Select 3 or 4 of your favorites from this list:
  - **Cauliflower florets**
  - **Green pepper rings**
  - **Cherry tomatoes**
  - **Carrot sticks**
  - **Celery sticks**
  - **Raw mushrooms**
  - **Broccoli florets**
  - **Lettuce leaves, washed and dried**
  - **Wonder Dip (recipe follows)**

EQUIPMENT:
- Large plate *or* platter

1. Ask an adult to help you with cleaning and cutting the assorted vegetables into bite-sized pieces.
2. Line a large plate with lettuce leaves.
3. Arrange the vegetables over the lettuce in a pretty design. Leave a space in the middle for a small bowl of Wonder Dip.

Wonder Dip

Makes 1½ cups

INGREDIENTS:
- **1 cup sour cream**
- **½ cup plain yogurt**
- **1 package (½ ounce) green onion dip mix**

EQUIPMENT:
- **Small mixing bowl**
- **Rubber spatula**
- **Small serving bowl**

1. Combine sour cream and yogurt in a small mixing bowl.
2. Blend in the dip mix with a rubber spatula.
3. Spoon into small serving bowl and place on a vegetable platter.

SERVING TIP: Wash a large green pepper. Remove the stem end with a small sharp knife. Discard the seeds. Serve the dip in the green pepper "bowl."

Smart Snacks with Wonder Dip, this page;
Pizza Planks, Zebra Parfaits, page 48.

48 SPECIAL MENUS

Pizza Planks

Makes 6 servings

INGREDIENTS:
- 1 loaf (12 inches) French bread
- 1 jar (12 ounces) spaghetti sauce
- 1 package (4 ounces) sliced pepperoni
- 1 jar (2½ ounces) sliced mushrooms, drained
- 12 ounces shredded mozzarella cheese
- 2 tablespoons grated Parmesan cheese

EQUIPMENT:
- Cutting board
- Serrated knife
- 2 microwave-safe plates

1. Ask an adult to assist you in splitting the loaf of bread. Place the bread on a cutting board. Carefully split bread in half lengthwise. Remove some of the soft bread to make a slightly hollowed loaf.
2. Place each half on a plate, cut-sides-up. Spoon spaghetti sauce evenly over both halves. Arrange pepperoni, mushrooms, and mozzarella cheese evenly over the tops. Sprinkle with Parmesan cheese.
3. Microwave each pizza separately on HIGH for 1½ minutes. Rotate the plate a quarter-turn.
4. Microwave on HIGH for another 1 to 1½ minutes, until cheese is bubbly.

Note: Use your imagination when making Pizza Planks. Add your favorite ingredients — green peppers, onions, cooked sausage, and hotdogs are a few suggestions.

Zebra Parfaits

Makes 4 servings

INGREDIENTS:
- 1 box (3½ ounces) chocolate pudding mix, *do not use instant*
- 2 cups milk
- 1 carton (4 ounces) refrigerated whipped topping
- 4 stemmed maraschino cherries, optional

EQUIPMENT:
- 4 parfait glasses
- Spoon

1. Prepare the chocolate pudding with 2 cups milk; follow the recipe on page 44.
2. When the pudding has cooled, layer it with the whipped topping in parfait glasses. Start with chocolate pudding and finish with whipped topping. There should be about three layers of each.
3. Top each serving with a cherry.

SPECIAL MENUS 49

IT'S A PICNIC!
My Hero (page 50)
Deviled Eggs in the Grass (page 50)
Potato Chips   Pickles
Big Red Apples
Crunch Munch Treats (page 49)

Crunch Munch Treats

Makes 2 dozen

INGREDIENTS:
- 1 tablespoon butter
- 1 package (14 ounces) caramels
- 3 tablespoons water
- 1 cup crisp corn cereal squares
- 1 cup bran cereal squares
- 1 cup crispy rice cereal
- 1 cup granola
- ½ cup shredded coconut
- 1½ cups salted peanuts
- ½ cup milk chocolate chips
- 1 tablespoon shortening

EQUIPMENT:
- 9 x 13-inch glass baking dish
- Paper towels
- 1-quart batter bowl
- Wooden spoon
- Measuring cups and spoons
- Large mixing bowl
- Tablespoon
- 1-cup glass measure

1. Lightly butter the baking dish. (To do this, put butter in the dish and push it around with a paper towel. It will leave a thin layer of butter on the bottom and keep the cookies from sticking.)

2. Remove caramel wrappings. Place the caramels in a batter bowl; add water. Microwave on HIGH for 1½ minutes; stir with a wooden spoon. Microwave on HIGH for another 1½ to 2 minutes, until caramels are melted.

3. Combine the cereals, granola, coconut, and peanuts in a large mixing bowl; toss together.

4. Carefully pour the caramel over the cereals. Stir gently until all the pieces are evenly coated. Pour into the buttered dish. Spread a little butter on the back of a tablespoon and gently press the mixture evenly into the dish.

5. Microwave the chocolate chips and shortening in a glass measure on HIGH for 1 minute; stir. Microwave on HIGH for 1 to 1½ minutes more, until chocolate is melted.

6. Very slowly drizzle the chocolate over the cereal mixture, making thin lines across the top.

7. Chill about 30 minutes or until chocolate is set.

8. Cut into squares.

50 SPECIAL MENUS

My Hero

Makes 1 generous serving

INGREDIENTS:
- 1 submarine roll, partially split
- 2 tablespoons mayonnaise
- 1 slice American cheese, cut in half diagonally
- 2 to 3 thin slices roast beef
- 2 thin slices fully cooked ham
- 1 slice salami, cut in half
- ½ slice mozzarella cheese, cut in half diagonally
- 4 dill pickle slices
- 3 black olives, sliced
- Lettuce leaves
- Red onion slices, optional

EQUIPMENT:
- Table knife
- Paper towel

1. Place the split roll on a paper towel. Open it so it will lay flat; spread with mayonnaise.
2. Place the American cheese halves on the roll bottom, with the points extending out.
3. Roll up the beef slices and place on the roll.
4. Roll up the ham slices and place on the roll.
5. Add the salami halves.
6. Top with mozzarella cheese.
7. Sprinkle with pickle slices and olive slices.
8. Wrap in a paper towel and microwave on HIGH for 30 seconds. Turn the sandwich a half-turn.
9. Microwave on HIGH for 20 to 35 seconds, until cheese begins to melt. Remove from microwave. Let stand 1 minute.
10. Add lettuce leaves and onions, if desired.

Deviled Eggs in the Grass

Makes 1 dozen

INGREDIENTS:
- 6 hard-boiled eggs, peeled
- 2 tablespoons mayonnaise
- 1 tablespoon mustard
- ¼ teaspoon salt
- 3 olives, halved
- 1 container (4 ounces) alfalfa sprouts

EQUIPMENT:
- 1 styrofoam egg carton
- Paring knife
- Small cutting board
- Small mixing bowl
- Fork
- Measuring spoons
- Teaspoon

1. In hot soapy water, wash the styrofoam egg carton. Rinse in hot water and dry. Set aside.
2. Cut eggs in half horizontally on a cutting board. Gently remove the yolks and place them in a small mixing bowl; save the whites.
3. Mash the yolks with a fork. Add the mayonnaise, mustard, and salt; mix until smooth.
4. Using a teaspoon, carefully return the yolk mixture back into the whites. Top with olive halves.
5. Open the egg carton and arrange alfalfa sprouts in each of the egg holders, with the green portion up. Carefully place deviled eggs on the sprouts.

NOTE: These eggs are perfect to take on a picnic! Simply close the egg carton and they are ready to go!

Crunch Munch Treats, page 49; Deviled Eggs in the Grass, My Hero, this page

SPECIAL MENUS

A MEXICAN FIESTA
Macho Nachos (page 53)
Confetti Salad (page 53)
Mexican Lasagna (page 52)

Mexican Lasagna

Makes 6 to 8 servings

INGREDIENTS:
- 1 pound very lean ground beef
- 1 package (1¼ ounces) taco seasoning mix
- 1 can (8 ounces) tomato sauce
- 1 can (15 ounces) kidney beans, drained
- 4 8-inch flour tortillas, halved
- 1 cup shredded Cheddar cheese
- 1 cup shredded Monterey Jack cheese

EQUIPMENT:
- 2-quart batter bowl
- Paper towel
- Wooden spoon
- Potholders
- 12 x 8-inch glass baking dish
- Waxed paper

1. Place the ground beef in a batter bowl. Cover with a paper towel. Microwave on HIGH for 3 minutes. Stir with a wooden spoon. Microwave on HIGH for 2 to 3 more minutes, until the meat is no longer pink.

2. Carefully remove the bowl from the oven, using potholders.

3. Add the taco seasoning mix, tomato sauce, and kidney beans; stir.

4. Layer four of the tortilla halves on the bottom of the baking dish, with straight sides along the outside and curved sides facing the center.

5. Spread half the meat mixture over the tortillas. Sprinkle with half the Cheddar cheese and half the Monterey Jack cheese.

6. Cover with the remaining tortilla halves.

7. Spread with the remaining meat mixture. Sprinkle with the rest of the cheeses.

8. Cover with waxed paper and microwave on HIGH for 5 minutes. Rotate dish a quarter-turn.

9. Microwave on HIGH for 4 to 5 more minutes, until it is hot throughout and the cheese is melted.

10. With potholders, carefully remove from the microwave.

11. Let stand 10 to 15 minutes before serving.

SPECIAL MENUS

Macho Nachos

Makes 1 dozen

INGREDIENTS:
- 12 round tortilla chips
- 1 can (3⅛ ounces) bean dip
- ½ cup shredded Cheddar cheese
- Mild taco sauce, optional
- Sour cream, optional
- Guacamole, optional

EQUIPMENT:
- Paper towel
- Microwave-safe plate
- ½ teaspoon measure

1. Place a paper towel on a plate.
2. Arrange the chips in a single layer over the paper towel.
3. Top each chip with ½ teaspoon of the bean dip.
4. Sprinkle with Cheddar cheese.
5. Microwave on HIGH for 30 seconds. Turn the plate a half-turn.
6. Microwave for 15 to 30 seconds more, until the cheese is completely melted.
7. Carefully remove from the microwave.
8. Serve Macho Nachos with taco sauce, sour cream, or guacamole, if desired.

Confetti Salad

Makes 6 servings

INGREDIENTS:
- 1 small head lettuce, torn into bite-sized pieces
- ⅓ cup sliced black olives
- 1 avocado, cut into wedges
- 1 large tomato, cut into wedges
- 1 cup shredded Cheddar cheese
- Round tortilla chips
- 1 bottle (8 ounces) taco salad dressing

EQUIPMENT:
- Large shallow salad bowl
- Measuring cups

1. Put the lettuce in the salad bowl.
2. Sprinkle with black olives.
3. Arrange avocado wedges over the salad like wheel spokes.
4. Place tomato wedges between the avocado slices.
5. Sprinkle with shredded cheese.
6. Tuck tortilla chips vertically around the edge of the bowl.
7. To serve, add the salad dressing at the table and toss. Or, carefully transfer salad to individual salad plates, and pass the dressing.

SMACKIN' GOOD SNACKS

Butterscotch Banana Pops

Makes 4 servings

INGREDIENTS:
- 2 ripe medium bananas, peeled
- ¾ cup butterscotch chips
- 2 tablespoons peanut butter
- ½ cup chopped salted peanuts

EQUIPMENT:
- Small knife
- 4 wooden popsicle sticks
- Plate
- Plastic wrap
- 2-cup glass measure
- Teaspoon
- Table knife
- Plastic bag

1. Cut each banana in half. Insert a popsicle stick into each half where it was cut. Place on a plate, cover with plastic wrap, and freeze until firm.
2. Place butterscotch chips in a 2-cup measure and microwave on HIGH for 1 minute; stir with a teaspoon. Add the peanut butter and stir again.
3. Microwave on HIGH for 30 to 60 seconds longer, until melted. Remove from microwave.
4. Remove bananas from freezer; dip into the melted butterscotch, rotating banana to coat. Smooth the coating all over with a table knife.
5. *Quickly,* roll each banana in chopped peanuts.
6. To store, place banana pops in a plastic bag and return to freezer.

Variations

- **Double Peanutty Pops:** Substitute peanut butter chips for the butterscotch chips.
- **Chocolate Peanutty Banana Pops:** Substitute semi-sweet chocolate chips for the butterscotch chips.

S'more 'n More

Makes 1 serving

INGREDIENTS:
- 2 graham cracker squares
- 1 tablespoon marshmallow cream
- 1 teaspoon mini chocolate chips
- 1 tablespoon peanut butter

EQUIPMENT:
- Paper towel
- Measuring spoons

1. Place 1 cracker square on a paper towel. Spoon the marshmallow cream in the middle of the cracker.
2. Sprinkle with chocolate chips.
3. Microwave on HIGH for 10 seconds, or until the marshmallow cream spreads close to the cracker edges. Remove from the microwave.
4. Spread the remaining graham cracker square with peanut butter; place over the other cracker square. Let stand for 1 minute.

Butterscotch Banana Pops (Chocolate Peanutty Variation), this page; Cookiepops, Chocolate Covered Pretzels, page 56; Crown Jewels, page 57.

SMACKIN' GOOD SNACKS

Cookiepops

Makes 10 pops

INGREDIENTS:

20 vanilla wafers
2 tablespoons creamy peanut butter
¾ cup pink *or* yellow summer coating pieces

EQUIPMENT:

Waxed paper
Cookie sheet
Teaspoon
10 wooden popsicle sticks
2-cup glass measure
Table knife *or* small rubber spatula

1. Place a piece of waxed paper on a cookie sheet. Lay 10 vanilla wafers on the waxed paper, flat-side-up. Spread each with about ½ teaspoon peanut butter.
2. Place a popsicle stick on the peanut butter. Top with the remaining cookies, pressing down to make 10 cookiepops.
3. Microwave the summer coating pieces in a glass measure on HIGH for 1 minute. Stir with a small rubber spatula.
4. Microwave on HIGH for 1 to 1¼ minutes, until melted. Stir until smooth.
5. Use a table knife to spread the coating on top of each cookiepop. Place the cookie sheet in the refrigerator for a few minutes, until coating is hard.
6. Turn the cookiepops over; spread the other side with the melted coating. If the coating mixture has cooled and thickened too much, warm it again on HIGH for 30 seconds and stir.

TIP: These can be made without the popsicle sticks, too.

Chocolate Covered Pretzels

Makes 25 pretzels

INGREDIENTS:

1 cup semi-sweet chocolate chips
2 teaspoons vegetable shortening
25 twisted pretzels
½ cup chopped nuts, optional

EQUIPMENT:

Small glass mixing bowl
Measuring cup and spoons
Rubber spatula
Waxed paper

1. Combine chocolate chips and shortening in a mixing bowl. Microwave on HIGH for 1 minute; stir with a rubber spatula.
2. Microwave on HIGH for 1 to 1½ minutes, until melted; stir until smooth.
3. Carefully remove chocolate from microwave.
4. Place a sheet of waxed paper on the counter near the bowl of melted chocolate.
5. Dip pretzels into the melted chocolate and place on the waxed paper.
6. If you like, sprinkle with chopped nuts.
7. Let pretzels stand at room temperature until the chocolate hardens, about 1 hour; or place in refrigerator for about 15 minutes.

Crown Jewels

Makes 1 dozen

INGREDIENTS:

12 marshmallows
¾ cup coarsely chopped salted peanuts
½ cup peanut butter chips
1 to 1½ tablespoons strawberry *or* grape jelly

EQUIPMENT:

Waxed paper
Custard cup
1-cup glass measure
Fork
Small spoon

1. Place marshmallows on a piece of waxed paper.
2. Pour the chopped peanuts into a small custard cup.
3. Pour the peanut butter chips into a glass measure. Microwave on HIGH for 1 minute; stir.
4. Microwave on HIGH for 30 seconds; stir.
5. Microwave for another 15 to 30 seconds on HIGH, until melted and hot; remove from microwave.
6. Stick a fork into the bottom of a marshmallow. Dip about one-half of it into the melted peanut butter morsels; then dip it in the peanuts. Place the marshmallow, dipped-end-up, on waxed paper.
7. Top with about ¼ teaspoon of jelly.
8. Repeat with the remaining marshmallows.
9. Let Crown Jewels dry on the waxed paper, about 20 minutes.

Granola

Makes about 5½ cups

INGREDIENTS:

½ cup butter
½ cup honey
3 cups oats
¾ cup sunflower nuts
1 cup coarsely chopped peanuts
½ cup wheat germ
½ cup brown sugar
½ cup raisins

EQUIPMENT:

2-cup glass measure
Measuring cups
3-quart glass mixing bowl
Wooden spoon
Potholders
Cookie sheet
Covered container

1. Microwave butter on HIGH in glass measure for 30 to 40 seconds, until melted. Remove from the microwave; add the honey.
2. Place oats, sunflower nuts, peanuts, wheat germ, and brown sugar in a mixing bowl.
3. Add the melted butter and honey.
4. Mix well with a wooden spoon.
5. Microwave on HIGH for 4 minutes; stir.
6. Microwave on HIGH for 2 minutes; stir.
7. Microwave on HIGH for 1 minute. Add the raisins; stir.
8. Microwave on HIGH for 1 more minute, or until the mixture is toasty; stir.
9. With potholders, carefully remove from the microwave. Pour on a cookie sheet; spread with the back of a wooden spoon. When cool, store in a covered container.

SMACKIN' GOOD SNACKS 59

Pop-a-Pizza

Makes 4 servings

INGREDIENTS:
- 4 English muffins, split and toasted
- 4 slices salami lunch meat
- 1 can (10½ ounces) pizza sauce
- 8 ounces mozzarella cheese, shredded
- Chopped green peppers, optional
- Cooked sausage, optional
- Black olives, optional
- Parmesan cheese, optional

EQUIPMENT:
- 2 microwave-safe plates
- Paper towels
- Cutting board
- Pizza cutter
- Tablespoon

1. Line plates with paper towels. Place 4 English muffin halves on each plate.
2. Stack the salami slices on a small cutting board. Cut the salami into thin long strips, using a pizza cutter. Then cut each strip in half; set aside.
3. Spread 1 or 2 tablespoons pizza sauce over each muffin half.
4. Divide salami strips evenly over the muffin halves.
5. Sprinkle generously with mozzarella cheese.
6. Microwave each plate on HIGH for 1½ to 2 minutes, until the cheese is bubbly. Serve immediately.
7. Decorate with remaining ingredients, if desired.

Nutty Haystacks

Makes 3 dozen

INGREDIENTS:
- ½ cup white sugar
- ½ cup white corn syrup
- ½ cup peanut butter
- 2 cups Chinese noodles
- ½ cup salted peanuts

EQUIPMENT:
- 1-quart batter bowl
- Measuring cups
- Wooden spoon
- Teaspoon
- Waxed paper, 18 inches long

1. Combine sugar and corn syrup in a batter bowl; stir with a wooden spoon. Microwave on HIGH 1½ minutes; stir. Microwave on HIGH for 1 to 2 minutes, until the mixture comes to a full boil. Carefully remove from microwave.
2. Stir the mixture with the wooden spoon. Add the peanut butter; stir until melted and completely blended.
3. Add the noodles and peanuts; stir until coated.
4. Use a teaspoon to drop the cookies on a sheet of waxed paper. They will become firm in 15 or 20 minutes.

Mexican Munch Olé, page 63; Nutty Haystacks, Pop-a-Pizza, this page; Granola, page 57.

60 SMACKIN' GOOD SNACKS

Brownies

Makes 16 brownies

INGREDIENTS:
- ½ cup butter *or* margarine
- 1 cup sugar
- 2 eggs
- ⅓ cup cocoa
- ¾ cup flour
- 2 teaspoons vanilla
- ½ cup chopped walnuts, if desired

EQUIPMENT:
- 8-inch square glass baking dish
- 2-quart batter bowl *or* medium mixing bowl
- Measuring cups and spoons
- Wooden spoon
- Paper towel
- Toothpick
- Potholders

1. Place butter in the baking dish. Microwave on HIGH for 1 minute, or until the butter is completely melted.
2. Carefully pour the butter into a batter bowl. Set the baking dish aside.
3. Add the sugar, eggs, and cocoa to the melted butter; mix well with a wooden spoon.
4. Add flour, vanilla, and chopped nuts, if desired; mix well with the wooden spoon.
5. Pour batter into the buttery baking dish.
6. Cover with a paper towel, and microwave on HIGH for 5 to 7 minutes, or until a toothpick inserted in the center comes out clean. Rotate the dish after 3 minutes for more even cooking.
7. With potholders, remove from microwave. Cool completely before cutting into 1-inch squares.

Zippy Dip

Makes 1½ cups

INGREDIENTS:
- 2 packages (3 ounces each) cream cheese
- ¼ cup **vegetable juice** *or* **tomato juice**
- ⅔ cup sour cream
- 1 package (⁷⁄₁₀ ounce) dry Italian salad dressing mix
- Fresh raw vegetables *or* chips

EQUIPMENT:
- 2-cup glass measure
- Measuring cups
- Fork

1. Place the cream cheese in a glass measure. Microwave on HIGH for 30 to 45 seconds, until cheese is softened. Remove from the microwave.
2. Add vegetable juice, sour cream, and Italian dressing mix; mix well with a fork. Serve immediately or cover and chill until serving.
3. Serve with fresh raw vegetables, cut into bite-sized pieces, or chips.

SMACKIN' GOOD SNACKS

Chili con Queso Dip

Makes 1 cup

INGREDIENTS:
- 8 ounces American cheese, cubed
- 2 tablespoons milk
- 2 tablespoons mild picante sauce
- Corn chips

EQUIPMENT:
- Measuring spoons
- 1-quart batter bowl

1. Place cheese and milk in a batter bowl. Microwave on HIGH for 1½ minutes; stir.
2. Add the picante sauce and stir.
3. Microwave on HIGH for another 30 to 45 seconds, until the cheese is completely melted.
4. Serve as a dip with corn chips.

NOTE: For a spicier dip, simply add more picante sauce.

Speedy Nachos

Makes 1 serving

INGREDIENTS:
- Tortilla chips
- ½ cup shredded Cheddar cheese

EQUIPMENT:
- Paper plate
- ½-cup measure

1. Spread chips in a single layer on a paper plate; completely cover the plate.
2. Sprinkle evenly with cheese.
3. Microwave on HIGH for 30 to 45 seconds, just until the cheese melts.

Inside Out Sandwich

Makes 1 serving

INGREDIENTS:
- 1 thin slice lean ham luncheon meat
- ¼ teaspoon mustard
- 1 slice Swiss cheese
- 1 Italian breadstick

EQUIPMENT:
- Paper plate
- Table knife
- Toothpick
- Paper towel

1. Place ham slice on a paper plate.
2. Spread with mustard.
3. Center the cheese over the ham.
4. Place a breadstick at one end of the cheese-ham stack and roll up. Secure with a toothpick.
5. Return to the paper plate with the seam side down. Cover loosely with a paper towel. Microwave on HIGH for 20 to 25 seconds, until the cheese is melted.
6. Let stand 1 minute. Remove the toothpick before serving.

SMACKIN' GOOD SNACKS

Mexican Munch Olé

Makes about 8 cups

INGREDIENTS:
- ½ cup butter
- 1 tablespoon taco seasoning mix
- 2 cups corn chips
- 2 cups crisp corn cereal squares
- 1 cup crisp rice cereal squares
- 1 cup peanuts
- 2 cups pretzel sticks

EQUIPMENT:
- 1-cup glass measure
- Fork
- Measuring cups and spoons
- 9 x 13-inch glass baking dish
- Potholders

1. Put butter in a glass measure. Microwave on HIGH for 1 minute, or until butter is melted. Remove from microwave. Stir in the taco seasoning mix with a fork; set aside.
2. Combine the corn chips, cereals, pretzels, and peanuts in the baking dish.
3. Drizzle with the butter mixture; stir with a fork.
4. Microwave on HIGH for 2 minutes. Open the oven door and stir the mixture with a fork. Microwave on HIGH for another 1 to 2 minutes, until heated through.
5. With potholders, remove from the oven. Cool before serving.
6. Store any leftover Mexican Munch in a sealed glass jar or plastic bag.

The Super Smacker

Makes 2 super smackers

INGREDIENTS:
- 20 marshmallows
- 3 tablespoons butter
- ½ cup semi-sweet chocolate chips
- 3 cups crisp rice cereal
- Additional butter

EQUIPMENT:
- Measuring cups and spoons
- 2-quart batter bowl *or* 2-quart microwave-safe bowl
- Wooden spoon
- 2 12 x 12-inch squares waxed paper
- 2 12 x 12-inch squares aluminum foil

1. Combine marshmallows, butter, and chocolate chips in a batter bowl. Microwave on HIGH for 1 minute. The marshmallows will puff up; stir the mixture down with a wooden spoon. Microwave on HIGH for another 20 to 30 seconds, until marshmallows and chocolate chips are completely melted.
2. Carefully remove the bowl from the microwave. Add the cereal; stir with a wooden spoon until completely coated.
3. Pour half the cereal mixture onto a square of waxed paper.
4. Lightly butter hands; shape the mixture into a large candy-cone shape, rounded at the base and pointed at the top. Shape the remaining mixture the same way.
5. Let the smackers dry until no longer sticky, about 20 or 30 minutes. Wrap each smacker in foil, twisting at the top to resemble candy kisses.

The Super Smacker, this page.

INDEX

BREAKFASTS TO BRAG ABOUT
Apple Honeys, 16
Breakfast Burrito, 12
Breakfast Pizza, 9
Crisp Bacon Slices, 11
Egg Ragamuffin, 15
Fruit Kebob, 11
Go Power Muffins, 17
Hot Chocolate, 12
Scrambled Eggs, 15
Sugar 'n Spice Grapefruit, 13
Topsy Turvy Apple Pancake, 13
Walking Breakfast, 11

DAZZLING DESSERTS
Cherry Crisp Cups, 44
Chocolate Pudding from a Mix, 44
Strawberry Shortcakes, 43
Triple Chocolate Cupcakes, 45

GETTING STARTED
Before You Cook, 8
Cooking Gear, 6
Measuring Equivalents, 8
Microwave Tips, 5
Playing it Safe, 4

MARVELOUS MAIN MEALS
Chicken and Rice, 20
Easy Meat Loaf Ring, 25
Garlic Bread, 22
Gold Nuggets, 24
Italian Squiggles, 20
Old Wagon Wheel Dinner, 21
Super Supper Nachos, 22
Wild West Chili, 18
Zesty Drumsticks, 18

SENSATIONAL SALADS
Berry Good Salad, 32
Double Red Salad, 31
Fruit 'n Bubbles, 32
Marinated Bean Salad, 33
Unbelievable Salad, 31

SMACKIN' GOOD SNACKS
Brownies, 60
Butterscotch Banana Pops, 54
Chili con Queso Dip, 61
Chocolate Covered Pretzels, 56
Cookiepops, 56
Crown Jewels, 57
Granola, 57
Inside Out Sandwich, 61
Mexican Munch Olé, 63
Nutty Haystacks, 59
Pop-a-Pizza, 59
S'more 'n More, 54
Speedy Nachos, 61
The Super Smacker, 63
Zippy Dip, 60

SPECIAL MENUS
It's a Picnic, 49
Crunch Munch Treats, 49
Deviled Eggs in the Grass, 50
My Hero, 50

A Mexican Fiesta, 52
Confetti Salad, 53
Macho Nachos, 53
Mexican Lasagna, 52

The Pizza Party, 47
Pizza Planks, 48
Smart Snacks, 47
Zebra Parfaits, 48

SUPER SANDWICHES
Ball Park Hotdogs, 34
Catch-of-the-Day, 38
Coney Fiesta Dog, 37
Dip 'n Sip, 36
Flash Burgers, 40
Fiesta Burgers, 37
Fish-n-Boats, 34
Sloppy Joes, 40
Tacos, 38
The Lunch Club, 36
Tower of Pizza, 41

VERSATILE VEGETABLES
Baked Potato, 29
Best Baked Beans, 29
Broccoli — Gee Whiz, 28
Corn on the Cob, 28
Green Beans in a Snap, 27
Space Spuds, 27